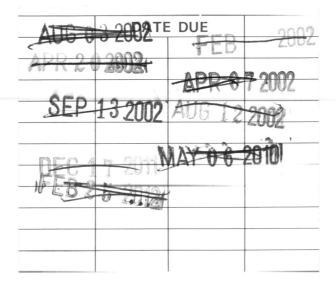

Verbs

Kelly Doudna

3102
Center for children's books

Published by SandCastle™, an imprint of ABDO Publishing Company, 4940 Viking Drive, Edina, Minnesota 55435.

Printed in the United States.

Photo credits: Comstock, Digital Stock, Eyewire Images, PhotoDisc, Rubber Ball

Library of Congress Cataloging-in-Publication Data

Doudna, Kelly, 1963-
    Verbs / Kelly Doudna.
      p. cm. -- (Sentences)
    Includes index.
    ISBN 1-57765-615-6
     1. English language--Verb--Juvenile literature. [1. English language--Verb.] I. Title.

PE1271 .D66 2001
428.2--dc21

                           2001022892

The SandCastle concept, content, and reading method have been reviewed and approved by a national advisory board including literacy specialists, librarians, elementary school teachers, early childhood education professionals, and parents.

Let Us Know

After reading the book, SandCastle would like you to tell us your stories about reading. What is your favorite page? Was there something hard that you needed help with? Share the ups and downs of learning to read. We want to hear from you! To get posted on the Abdo Publishing Company Web site, send us email at:

sandcastle@abdopub.com

About SandCastle™

Nonfiction books for the beginning reader

- Basic concepts of phonics are incorporated with integrated language methods of reading instruction. Most words are short, and phrases, letter sounds, and word sounds are repeated.

- Readability is determined by the number of words in each sentence, the number of characters in each word, and word lists based on curriculum frameworks.

- Full-color photography reinforces word meanings and concepts.

- "Words I Can Read" list at the end of each book teaches basic elements of grammar, helps the reader recognize the words in the text, and builds vocabulary.

- Reading levels are indicated by the number of flags on the castle.

Note: Some pages in this book contain more than ten words in order to more clearly convey the concept of the book.

Look for more SandCastle books in these three reading levels:

Level 1 (one flag)	Level 2 (two flags)	Level 3 (three flags)

Grades Pre-K to K 5 or fewer words per page	**Grades K to 1** 5 to 10 words per page	**Grades 1 to 2** 10 to 15 words per page

Verbs

A verb is an action or being word.

Verbs

We skate along the path with Mom.

Verbs

We sit on the dock and fish all afternoon.

Verbs

I play in the snow and slide down the hill.

Verbs

I practice for my piano lesson.

I get better every week.

Verbs

I found two beetles.

They crawl around on the deck.

Verbs

I read with my friend.

He is smart.

Verbs

I call my friend.

We chat for several minutes.

Verbs

What do I do at the park?

(hit, play, swing)

Words I Can Read

Nouns

A noun is a person, place, or thing

afternoon (af-tur-NOON) p. 9
beetles (BEE-tuhlz) p. 15
deck (DEK) p. 15
dock (DOK) p. 9
friend (FREND) pp. 17, 19
hill (HIL) p. 11
park (PARK) p. 21
path (PATH) p. 7
piano lesson (pee-AN-oh LESS-uhn) p. 13
snow (SNOH) p. 11
verb (VURB) p. 5
week (WEEK) p. 13
word (WURD) p. 5

Plural Nouns

A plural noun is more than one person, place, or thing

minutes (MIN-itss) p. 19

Verbs

A verb is an action or being word

call (KAWL) p. 19
chat (CHAT) p. 19
crawl (KRAWL) p. 15
do (DOO) p. 21
fish (FISH) p. 9
found (FOUND) p. 15
get (GET) p. 13
hit (HIT) p. 21

is (IZ) pp. 5, 17
play (PLAY) pp. 11, 21
practice (PRAK-tiss) p. 13
read (REED) p. 17
sit (SIT) p. 9
skate (SKAYT) p. 7
slide (SLIDE) p. 11
swing (SWING) p. 21

Adjectives

An adjective describes something

action (AK-shuhn) p. 5
all (AWL) p. 9
being (BEE-ing) p. 5
every (EV-ree) p. 13

my (MYE) pp. 13, 17, 19
several (SEV-ur-uhl) p. 19
smart (SMART) p. 17
two (TOO) p. 15

Match each picture to the verb that describes the action happening in it

crawl

fish

sit

skate